A Somatic Sex Edu

TRAUMA:
A Practical Guide
to Working with
Body & Soul

Christiane Pelmas

The
ReWilding
Press
words for the wild human

ISBN: 978-1545212059

www.ChristianePelmas.com

cover photo: John Rocha CCO License

DEDICATION

This series is dedicated to the pioneering hearts and souls who are cultivating a world of erotically intelligent, embodied humans despite the fact that by doing our vocation we risk criminal prosecution.

May we stand together, support one another and remember …
we are the sane ones!

CONTENTS

ACKNOWLEDGMENTS

This series would not exist without colleague and co-conspirator, Caffyn Jesse's tireless, patient and enthusiastic editorial expertise, technological guidance and irreverent humor.

INTRODUCTION

Since 1998 I've been a clinical supervisor for psychotherapists, loving the field of learning, group inquiry and reflection that is specific to the setting of group supervision. Shortly after my own certification in Sexological Bodywork, in 2008, I began offering supervision and mentorship for somatic sex educators. In this time, I've been paying close attention to the work we practitioners are being called to do. My own story finding my way into this field from traditional psychotherapy seems to parallel so many others' journeys into the work: that we are called through our clients or through the longing of our own inner aspects heretofore unacknowledged and unsupported, to learn a new way and live a life unfolded.

Back in 2007, with a full psychotherapy practice that looked, to the outside observer, to be fairly traditional, I was working with a few specific clients as they fervently longed to own fragmented, alienated aspects of their spirit and sexuality. As it often happens (that there are themes that are relevant to several of our clients at once, unbeknownst to each other) within the short span of perhaps a month these three clients each came, essentially, to the same moment in their work. From a place of true and well-deserved frustration, as I was dutifully trying to meet their needs while staying (at least marginally) within the confines of my psychotherapy licensure's demands of me, they threw their hands up and exclaimed some version of, "I'm pretty sure I just need you to touch me!" In distress, but knowing they were exactly right, I found the Certification in Sexological

Bodywork and went about the process of transitioning my practice over from traditionally parametered, licensed clinical private practice to my own version of the hybrid pioneering work we're all in the process of co-developing.

The innocent, fervent intelligence of our clients, driven by nothing less magnificent than our human longing for wholeness and meaning, continues to be a powerful source of inspiration to me. The confluent moments back in 2007 that had me seek out a new modality were just the beginning. It seems, if we are open to the innate intelligence that resides deep within each being, making space for its expression in our midst, in short order we find our front doorsteps festooned with entreaties and gifts in the form of humans and their precious, relentless longing. If we make of ourselves a welcoming, shame-free presence and with this, an invitation for everyone in our midst to listen to the longing deep within their souls, we will likely find ourselves in a rare and vital place; forever standing at the leading-edge of our own learning.

And it is from the recognition of this that I offer these practitioner handbooks. In my work supervising and mentoring somatic sex educators I find that – as you work to stay with the growing edge of your clients' healing and wholing – the language, skills and knowing required to do so can feel like standing at the edge of the ocean as the tide comes in and washes the ground out from beneath you! Moments in which you may feel you have an at-least-proficient grasp of the situation can shift like a hummingbird's path, and you suddenly find yourself in a land of no language and high intensity, flying by the seat of your pants. There are some places where flying by the seat of our pants is unavoidable. And there are others that we can likely predict. Each handbook offered comes from a place of this predicted need for care, and a desire to support each of you in the front lines of your practice where you are primarily in conversation with your own wisdom, soul and whatever form of Spirit is your particular guidance. In the uncharted terrain of this pioneering field, there is no reason to unnecessarily re-create the wheel.

As an example of this, it was fascinating for me to begin specifically asking somatic sex education practitioners to categorize their work with clients – into touch and non-touch sessions. If they had to quantify their work, what would they say? Many of you report that at least half, if not more, of your work with clients is non-touch oriented! This is a fascinating development to acknowledge, and one that feels extremely important to support. If half the work we do with clients is non-touch, it's safe to assume (and is anecdotally borne out in my conversations with practitioners) that much of this non-touch work involves talk, and a level of support that more closely resembles insight-oriented coaching and even, at times, dare I say…psychotherapy! Who knows where our field will go, since it is still in its very early stages. But somatic sex educators are not coaches or therapists, and (unless like me, you've also been trained as such) we are not ethically able to purvey ourselves as such. Yet despite this true and important ethical boundary, we are being called into the terrain of human healing, where hands-on work and psychotherapy intersect. We are called into the nature of soul-centric tending to the human psyche while holding the soma, quite literally, in our (gloved) hands.

It's critical that we remember; this is a beautiful, map-less field, the true and wild nature of which many of us did not foresee. Yet we have been asked, perhaps by the will of the world to continually find more wholeness, to diligently fashion ourselves into stewards of skillful, ethical invitation and permission. As many of us have already experienced, wound in desperate search for its wholeness, and wholeness in search of its allies, all have a nose for the sort of souls who become somatic sex educators. Given this, hands-on practitioners of erotic wellness must be prepared with language, skill and care. These books are an offering to that cause.

WHAT IS TRAUMA?

Trauma results from "an inescapable stressful event that overwhelms a person's existing coping mechanisms."
van der Kolk & Fisher

"Trauma occurs when an event creates an unresolved impact on an organism."
"Trauma is in the nervous system, not in the event."
Peter A. Levine

Yet.....

As somatic sex educators we understand that in many cultures around the world and certainly in the dominant cultures resulting from industrialization and westernization, simply being a sexual being brings with it a myriad of traumas. These traumas range from acute and identifiable to covert, diffuse and difficult to discern. It can come as no surprise that we live in a deeply (pathologically) gendered world as well. The desire of dominant culture to keep us conforming to the 'straight' and narrow contributes a baseline of sexual/gender trauma which we might just assume has been true for us all. Whether we've had the opportunity to turn towards this ubiquitous trauma or not, it is unlikely any of us has escaped its tentacles. Consider, for a moment, the process most of us enter during latency and adolescence, when we begin to more consciously notice and explore our sexual selves. Whether we live within a family culture of 'don't ask don't tell' when it comes to sexuality, or one of more extreme dominance and ridicule, the result can be the same; we learn to touch ourselves quickly, without presence and with the particular form of (dis)embodiment borne of believing we are doing something fundamentally wrong. The trauma associated with the dissonance between the innate and rightful pleasure our bodies are capable of, and a culture which tells us it's sinful and abhorrent to feel sexual pleasure is, in and of itself, a deeply felt, rarely tended to trauma.

All this makes it of particular importance that somatic sex educators at the very least familiarize ourselves with the terrain of trauma work because whether or not our clients present to us a specific story of known trauma we must start with a curiosity which stems from the assumption that simply being born into industrialized culture is a trauma to selfhood and eros in itself. And we must know that to be erotically well in industrialized culture is to be anomalous and blessed. Of course, that's where we come in, as pioneers in a field dedicated to the creation of erotically-well culture; one awake, present, permissioned and joyful body at a time.

There are many different types of trauma, as we can experience it throughout our lives. Some of them include:

- *Shock Trauma* – big single event trauma such as a rape or another form of physical assault

- *Developmental Trauma* – more on-going experiences such as neglect, physical, emotional or sexual abuse or shame

- *Vicarious (secondary) Trauma* – what we might take on as a result of living in intimate quarters with a person who is actively traumatized i.e., the partner of a veteran, the sibling of a child who was sexually assaulted

- *Intergenerational/Cultural Trauma* – the experience of many people whose cultural heritage includes mass rape, systemic discrimination, slaughter, epidemics, refugee situations. This includes the experience we have living within a global culture which largely vilifies freedom of expression and often responds to it with violent force particularly when it concerns our sexual, gender and erotic expression. In fact, we might consider the gendering process, unconscious and immediate upon birth, inherently traumatic, given that we are placed into either/or categories with blatant disregard for our own experience and individuality. Further, we can also consider the natural process, somewhere during latency and adolescence, that happens for most of us, of discovering our sexuality in a more overt and purposeful way, to be a place of quiet yet traumatic acculturation. It is often with great secrecy, lack of guidance and the addition of overt or covert shaming accompanying this moment that we make our way through.

- *Community Trauma* – sexual violence happens to communities as well as to individuals. When a woman of color is raped by a white police officer, for example, effects of the trauma will be felt through both of their communities. There are also large-scale community traumas, such as the AIDS crisis of the 1980's, which left the gay community deeply impacted.

The Particular Potential for Somatic Sex Educators, Who Work With the Body, Where Trauma Is Stored

Because, unlike trauma therapists, we work hands-on with the physical bodies in which trauma is stored, we have an extra interface with our clients that even somatically oriented talk-therapists do not have. But that also means we can inadvertently 'stumble into' trauma in the body, as we are helping our clients map, nourish and grow their arousal. While acute instances of trauma recollection are still rare, milder versions of this awakening, remembering process are likely happening regularly in our offices as we bring attention, care and touch to places, and in ways, that have not been touched perhaps ever, or only ever touched in ways that have harmed and/or shamed.

Resiliency Factors which help determine if an event will remain in the system as trauma

- *Relational health and support* – does this person have close friends and family who track and care about this person and their well-being? The more we engage in trauma research, the more we find that social support appears to be one of the very biggest predictors of a person's immediate integration of a stressful event. In our very isolated cultures, where strong community is rare, we as practitioners might become the sole source of true community for our clients. While we must work to encourage clients to build community, we also must acknowledge that it might start with their first experience of true community being their time with us.

- *Access to support* – does this person have access to the support often required to integrate the experiences of an acute event or on-going events into their overall experience of wellness? This includes having both the permission and the opportunity to discuss the events and specificities of the trauma with professionals and community/family and engage in healing activities.

- *Life factors* – the state of physical and mental health, age and presence of any disabilities which can conspire to isolate a person.

- *Attachment history* – does this person have a foundation of secure attachment? There is a general spectrum here, from secure to disorganized with ambivalent and avoidant being in the middle of the spectrum, for how a person will be likely to cope with trauma. For more conversation on Attachment in this handbook, refer to the section *Providing Secure Attachment In Our Relationships With Clients*.

- *Level of soulfulness* – or, a person's intimacy with their own core essence or *soul*. This is a requisite for true, mature adulthood and it is also a rare thing in industrialized culture. Knowing, and primarily caring for, one's unique essence and gifts is anathema to the survival of the current dominant culture, which goes to great pains to homogenize and shame original, unique thought and expression. When we live an ensouled life we are less likely to take things personally and more likely to handle difficult or painful events with a sense of equanimity and fundamental wellness even while we are tending to anger, grief and more.

- *Relationship with 'Spirit'* – whether 'god', 'the divine', a 'Higher Power' or any other name, if we use any word at all to refer to the sense many of us have of a greater, benevolent intelligence, we tend to have more resiliency when it comes to the unpredictable events life throws at us. Having a prioritized relationship with Spirit also dramatically increases the depth, maturity and level of intimacy in all our relationships. It contributes profoundly to our sovereignty (the experience we have that our rightness-of-being isn't at the whim or mercy of what others think of us; that we are free to bring our truth regardless of its popularity and that we will be able to manage whatever results come from bringing our truth).

- *Internal Resources* – this is one of the areas of mystery for us in attempting to determine who will and won't walk away from an event or an on-going situation un-traumatized or traumatized. There is no fool-proof equation or set of variables. While it is true that a person with a disorganized attachment style who is fairly isolated from community and family and doesn't have the means to get support is more likely to experience effects of trauma in their system as the result of an event, it is by no means a solid predictor. It is just as mysterious that certain children emerge from traumatic childhoods during which they experienced pervasive abuse and neglect with a fairly resilient sense of self and wellness.

The Autonomic Nervous System:

"Trauma" is the set of intertwined on-going symptoms that are residual physiological effects of an overwhelmingly stressful event stored *in the body*. To understand how we might go about assisting the unwinding of these symptoms and effects, it's important to understand the systems which are primarily responsible for responding to stress events. It's also important that we understand the systems responsible for bringing us back to a physiological state of rest and wellness. Not only do these interdependent systems respond to acute events and enable us to rest in the absence of threat, they are responsible for our capacity to relax into deep pleasure states and even tolerate and lean-in to sensations of erotic intensity.

In systems which have not had the opportunity to integrate an acute event, the on-going physical responses of the original threat do not simply cause physical sensations, but trigger complex emotional responses effecting a person's sense of safety, wellness and either calm or terror, security or danger. Even more, these systems signaling danger can be triggered anywhere, at any time, by a 'small', even unnoticed, thing that happens to remind the brain of a past experience. (See "Re-Traumatization").

As an example, one night a while back as my partner, Jeff, was getting ready for bed, he began removing his clothes as he had nearly every night of his 45 years of life. As his conscious brain would tell him, nothing out of the ordinary had happened prior to that moment, and yet, the mind is a fantastically vigilant thing and it caught something new: a particular 'snap' as the belt came out of its loop. A snap it hadn't heard perhaps for decades. In this split-second, a piece of his past was mysteriously stirred into the present. He was brought immediately back to his boyhood and the terror of living with a father who intermittently, with no apparent warning, would beat him with a belt, among other violations both emotional and physical. In that moment, so far from the original threat, familiar sensations of fear and helplessness coursed through his body. As he would recount later, equally startling was the immediacy of the event; how quickly he could be brought right back *'there'*, and the vulnerability of realizing that in one minute he could be standing in his bedroom, a grown man, and the next he could be back in his small body, feeling terrified and confused.

I was already in bed and, though I was watching him the whole time (we were in the midst of a conversation sharing about the events of that day, as I remember it), I didn't know what was happening until he paused and held his belt for a moment. Then I knew. What happened next was a profound thing to experience so intimately. And it is a thing that can seem a gesture of impossible luxury for a person who has not been given the opportunity to engage in their own trauma work. He slowly came to bed and, feeling his body in the warm sheets, in the safety of his own home, next to a person who cares for him deeply and is a protector of his wellness, he momentarily felt the uncontrollable feelings associated with the powerlessness of his childhood. He felt the boy of him, who is still able to be awakened, given certain physical triggers and perhaps a particular lack of resource in the moment. And then, breathing and grounding to the reality of his present circumstances (and safety), he found himself resourced enough to feel heartbroken and then curious about what sort of childhood his father must have experienced to necessitate him unleashing such a true terror on his own son. This level of wellness, compassion and self-care is a thing we all strive for in the work of unwinding past trauma. It was a beautiful thing to experience; the body's capacity to momentarily touch into such monumental darkness only to return, in short order, to a state of true wellness. This is the *pendulation* between the different branches of our nervous system that allow us to be resilient and well in the face of acute events.

Our most basic physical activities – from our breathing, our heart rate, salivation, swallowing, our pupil dilation, speed of voice, facial expressions and more – are functions of a complex network of neural response systems called the autonomic nervous system (ANS). The ANS is made up of three branches, two of which are of great importance to us in our work with clients; the sympathetic (SNS) and parasympathetic (PNS). Behavioral Neuroscientist, Stephen Porges, describes these two governing networks as the body's accelerator and the body's brake, respectively. The third branch of the ANS is the enteric system which is our gastrointestinal tract. While the enteric system is of great importance to our endocrine and immune fitness, mental acuity, general energy and so much more, we will not explore it further in this handbook.

The SNS is the responsive branch of the nervous system, reacting to environmental factors (perceived or measurable) with capacities that have, primarily, self-preservation in mind. In response to a threat the SNS dumps a cocktail of chemistry including adrenalin into the bloodstream. This serves to move blood to large muscle groups, increases our respiration, dilates our pupils (to let more light in and give us greater vision), increases our heart rate and blood pressure and much more. All these physiological responses are primal responses to perceived threat. We do not control these responses. They happen automatically. However, as you will see below, the SNS is not a steadfast impenetrable force of responsiveness. Given just the right input, repeatedly, over time, combined with the lack of opportunity to process or sequence that input through the system, the SNS will become over-sensitized to its environment.

The PNS is the slow and steady branch of the ANS. The rule of thumb, which perhaps you've read in other texts, is that the PNS is responsible for the "rest and digest" or "feed and breed" arm of our ANS. Importantly, the PNS and the SNS are designed to work harmoniously with each other and it is the PNS that triggers the SNS to come back to resting after a perceived threat is no longer present.

Of particular concern to us as somatic sex educators is the sensitization that can happen to the SNS, referenced above. One of the by-products of unresolved trauma in a body is that the SNS tends to run at a low-grade pitch all the time, as it has been repeatedly triggered into action, over and over again, each time a new event happens; like removing your belt at the end of the day. People who have not had help integrating their trauma are likely to be receiving messages of acute danger on a regular basis. Under the impression it is doing its job, the SNS triggers the physiological responses which prepare to deal with the (old) threat. Over time, the SNS' over-activity numbs the PNS, which in turn stops trying to slow the body down. The balance between these two systems, a balance critical to our sense of well-being and our capacity to respond in the moment to what is true rather than what is perceived, becomes skewed.

A person who lives in a body that is consistently sending fight or flight signals to the brain can easily and understandably create a story about the world from this place; that it is an unsafe place, that goodness and safety are not possible let alone the norm. This body and spirit would become one that largely exists in opposition to the stimulus that comes toward it, since *any* stimulus will begin to be seen as threatening. So much of our work, as it parallels trauma work, consists of helping a body and soul feel itself as a safe place where all emotions including joy, fear, anger and vulnerability are welcome and even wanted. Often our greatest gift to a client is helping to widen the range of possibility within their embodied experience, so they can begin to feel things without judgment and learn to intentionally expand pleasurable intensity without associating it with the negative intensity of early trauma.

Stephen Porges coined the term "neuroception" which refers to our nervous system's evaluation of risk, or, the process our neural circuits undergo to determine, in any given moment, whether we are safe, in danger or in a life-threatening situation. Our work with clients who are holding unresolved trauma requires that we not only help them more accurately evaluate each moment for its true threat factor but that we also, equally, help them to find states of ever-deepening relaxation, pleasure and well-being. This is why somatic sex educators are in a great position to help unwind traumatized bodies; because we assist our clients in finding, maintaining and growing their capacity for deep, relaxed, sustained pleasure.

Our Nervous Systems Have Not Evolved to Accommodate Current Experiences

While our brains have certainly evolved over the roughly 4 million years we've been learning to stand, use language and develop complex technology, they have not evolved enough to accommodate the myriad assaults to our psyche we experience on a near-daily basis. Things like pornography, the mainstream selections found in movie theatres, on TV and even the nightly news are all overwhelming experiences for a brain that evolved to field singular threat in a linear fashion, and not in such a barrage of volume and frequency as we have come to expect and even seek out. The last 50 years alone, and the three generations within it, have seen a tremendous increase in the baseline experience we seek in order to feel entertained as well as the level of violence we are now numbed to. Some people routinely see horror films and ride the roller coasters available at amusement parks because they have learned to harness the SNS's response, feeding off the chemicals of cortisol, norepinephrine and adrenaline as they are dumped into the bloodstream.

While the chemistry that supports our primal impulse for survival isn't meant to be the weekend's big entertainment, it's also important to know that the series of responses and interlocking physiological and emotional events is a brilliant and complex network designed to assure our survival and re-connect with our tribe; whose role in our safety and well-being is meant to be beneficent. The fact that most of us who are victims of violence will experience it at the hands of someone we know, and likely know well – a person who is often in charge of attending to our safety – is a tragic human development that our nervous system, particularly the social engagement branch of it, has not evolved to accommodate.

Of further interest, while our ANS was quite magnificently designed to respond to significant acute threat and assault, we are not designed to deal with the ravages of chronic stress. Of all the particular symptoms and effects that unresolved trauma might bring with it, the illnesses and disease that are caused by persistent stress offer particularly new threats to our wellbeing which neither our evolution nor modern medicine have caught up with. Here, somatic sex educators are at the front lines of the efficacy curve, as it is a particular focus of the profession to guide bodies, and the souls that inhabit them, into greater and more sustained states of pleasure and wellness. So far, this is the only lasting, holistic antidote to chronic stress.

THE SPECIFIC PROCESS: HOW & WHY TRAUMA GETS TRAPPED IN THE BODY

It's important to understand the specific events that do, and don't, happen in order for an event to be more likely to create trauma in a body.

Physiological Occurrences During a Life Threatening Event

- Increased heart rate

- Increase in respiration

- Increased adrenalin, cortisol and norepinephrine released into bloodstream

- Increased blood to larger muscles

- Increased hyper-vigilance

There Are Two Evolutionary Impulses in Humans When Faced With an Acute Event

- *Mobilizing* – moving, sequencing, metabolizing *fight or flight*

- *Contraction* – roots to a single cell organism and fetuses, *immobilize and freeze*. Along with the *freeze* response might come a secondary adaptive survival behavior, to *appease*. (See below for more on this important adaptive experience).

If the Body Is Unable to Fight or Flee

- The body FREEZES (and sometimes appeases)

- Additional chemistry gets dumped into the bloodstream to create numbing

- This is an intelligent and compassionate response; some predators won't eat prey if it appears to be dead (opossum), and it also helps numb us from the pain of an attack

- All of the fight/flight physiology is still active in the body, but there is no movement or action to sequence the energy. Some liken this to having our foot on the accelerator and the brake at the same time.

- If the freeze happens in a situation involving another human or humans, and there is an element of relationality to it, a secondary adaptive response can happen, called appeasing. Those who spend time with canines see this appeasing process anytime two dogs who do not know each other come together; it looks like the subordinate befriending behavior of grinning, licking the muzzle of the more-alpha animal and sometimes if all else fails to communicate ranking, the subordinate one will get on its back and present its belly. For humans who manage cultural expectations which values independence, personal autonomy and power-over, our instinct to appease can be particularly difficult to accept, because in hindsight we might imagine we didn't do everything we could to defend ourselves and overcome our aggressor. The *immobilize and freeze* response happens in a system which sees no reasonable way to avoid the imminent attack. When the imminent attack is by another human we have the option of bargaining in the form of appeasement; which includes a range of behaviors from a deferential facial expression to a long-term relationship of subservience and victimization. In every single case it is critical to remember, and to help our clients understand, that regardless of the depth and intricacy of the appeasement, nor the actual real threat to the client, appeasement is all the evidence needed to know that this person felt entirely without power or recourse to protect themselves. Once a person begins to gain safety and perspective around the events of their trauma, the shame that is often associated with the freeze and appease response can feel insurmountable at times. It is our job to help educate our clients to the brilliance of these adaptive behaviors that kept them safe, without which they would not be in our offices longing for more health.

- If the body is invited to respond instinctively to the presence of this level of chemistry and perceived threat to the system's survival, it will naturally shake, sweat, fart, burp, yawn and other motions and responses designed to move energy out of the system and regulate the SNS to resting respiration and heart rates. It's important to know that while talking, telling our story of trauma and being invited to be witnessed in the memories of an event are all important processes, they do not resolve trauma by themselves and in fact, they are not the necessary process to trauma resolution. The body's process of *releasing the stored energy that didn't have the opportunity to sequence through at the time of the event* is the critical process in all trauma resolution.

The Long-Term Effects of Unsequenced Trauma in The Body

- When the energy does not get processed or sequenced through the body, it remains held in the nervous system, creating a self-perpetrating cycle of continuous internal activation and re-activation.

- This, in turn, creates living responses in the body which are, by western medicine, often pejoratively called trauma 'disorders.' It is critical we learn to identify these various adaptive (short term), then maladaptive (long-term) behaviors in our clients so we can advocate for and help tend to their health and well-being. It is also imperative that we remember these symptoms-called-disorders are logical responses to dangerous and scary situations, as perceived by our clients. These behaviors are often the result of the body and psyche's attempt to create safety and order in an environment that feels anything *but* safe and ordered. These behaviors include, but are not limited to, Post Traumatic Stress Disorder, Dissociative Identity Disorder, anxiety, depression, obsessive/compulsive behavior, and more generalized symptoms including weight loss/gain, sleep difficulty/insomnia, compromised immune system and more susceptibility to illness and relational difficulties which might make maintaining long-term relationships (platonic and otherwise) more difficult.

- *Dissociation* – Perhaps one of the most common behaviors in the trauma family, dissociation simply refers to the capacity to sequester the normally integrated function of memory, sensation, perception, and identity when faced with emotional and/or physiological input that exceeds what a person can process. Fundamentally, dissociative behavior is highly adaptive and is often the mechanism that allows a child to keep parts of themselves safe in the face of deeply fracturing experiences. Over time however, dissociation can cause us to feel forgetful, foggy, disoriented, 'not really here' and, of course, numb to our bodies, which is often the symptom we, as somatic sex educators, encounter first.

- *Acute Dissociation* – also called 'shock', this form of dissociation is a brilliant adaptive response to an overwhelming moment or acute event. Typically 'shock' refers to the dissociation that happens directly after the event. I remember an experience with a client just shortly after I started doing somatic sex education work. I had been seeing this person for a few months regularly when, one day, she showed up about 20 minutes late for a session. She was out of breath but other than that, rather 'flat' and without emotion. Her face was a strange pale, almost ghostly blue-white color. She brushed past me in a dreamy sort of way and sat on the couch looking out the window as if nothing were out of the ordinary. Except she had never before been a second late for an appointment let alone twenty minutes! She sat just feet from me and yet she felt strangely far away. I noticed I was feeling out of sorts as well, though I hadn't been feeling this way prior to her arrival. It took me a few minutes to realize she was in shock. Calmly, I asked her what had her late to our session. Almost lackadaisically, and with a little laugh, she said, "oh, I hit a deer on my way over here." And with that, she turned her gaze back toward the window. In a neutral but curious way, I asked her some basic questions about her experience. With each answer, I felt *more of* her come into the room. Her color returned. Her posture shifted. She began making more eye contact with me. Slowly, over the course of our remaining seventy minutes, she came back to the present moment with access to her emotions and the full experience of the shocking event. Eventually she was able to shake, sob, breathe, jump up and down, swinging her arms from side to side, and more. All this was her body's natural response to the original event, free to come through once the shock began wearing off. While a person is in shock, it is our role to normalize their experience and create a space of calm and safety. If we do this, the natural progression of sequencing will often happen on its own.
- *Numbness, Lack of Capacity to Feel Pleasure, Anhedonia* – This is a version of dissociation but it merits its own bullet because of our field of inquiry and attention. We work in the realm of sexuality, arousal and pleasure. It is a common experience for clients to reach out to us because they are having trouble *feeling* or they are *feeling numbness*. The distinctions here are important. Perhaps a client *cannot ever* feel certain parts of their body; or these geographic areas go numb only when the client begins to feel aroused; or they specifically *cannot feel pleasure* (anhedonia) in their body or in specific parts of their body but they can feel other things, like pain.

While it is true that, at times, our clients may be suffering from the very natural physiological effects of scar tissue, it is (in my clinical experience) just as, if not more, likely they are experiencing the long-term effects of unsequenced trauma trapped in the body.

Re-Traumatization

When unsequenced trauma is left in the nervous system any subsequent stimuli that are remotely reminiscent of the original event – like removing one's belt at the end of the day – can re-trigger the SNS's entire physiological process, and any subsequent emotional processes that have been habituated will get retriggered as well. A person can live in this particular feedback loop, and the habits which grow around and inside this loop, for the entirety of their lives, without ever knowing they are caught there.

Embodied Memory & Neuroplasticity

It's important to remember, however, that memories do not get stored in impenetrable databanks. Current research illuminates the fluid and fluctuating state of the information we call memory. Further, we also now know that there is a thing called, **'embodied memory'**. Embodied memory is the information which lives not only in the muscle and tissue of our bodies, beyond and regardless of cognition, but the memory information living in our gestures, expressions and physical states-of-being (recall Jeff's experience as he removed his belt). Hopeful recent research on embodied memory and embodiment indicates we have the capacity to re-write our experience of an event by having a different physical experience *around* the memory of the event. In order to talk about how embodied memory pertains to our work, it is important to understand the brain's capacity for 'neuroplasticity'.

Neuroplasticity is the brain's ability to reorganize itself throughout a lifetime by forming new neural networks. Neuroplasticity can work *for* us and it can work *against* us. While it is true that the younger brain is vastly more neuroplastic than the adult brain, brains are neurologically responsive to external stimuli for the entirety of their lives. Even an adult brain free from unsequenced trauma in its youth can find itself creating the neural networks and embodied patterning of trauma when immersed in a situation of repeated terror and lack of safety. And the reverse is, fortunately, also true: a brain that was subjected to severe trauma in its youth can heal its neurological patterning given the right environment of safety and assistance. The fact that our brains have Neuroplasticity is what allows us to heal from trauma.

How can we work with embodied memory to take advantage of the endowment of neuroplasticity? Somatic sex educators are in the business of intelligent, embodied pleasure. Many of us are in this business specifically because we know pleasure is a powerful tool in our healing and sustained wholeness, not simply a good thing, or even our birthright. Specifically, we believe that the *act of feeling good* is both an intimately subversive and culturally subversive act. If more of us believed this about our pleasure not only might we have a lot less violence in the world and a whole lot more joy but as embodiment preachers and practitioners, we imagine that, with more presence and joy it is likely we would have a lot more wind turbines, rewilded green spaces for wild creatures to roam and thrive, less economic disparity and little or no addiction. As embodiment guides we bring an invitation to prioritize intelligent embodied pleasure into our sessions – with great care and repetition – as we gently and continuously remind our clients to orient to what feels good. We do this because we know the endogenous (internally created) chemistry of feeling good brings with it ever-increasing wellness as we experience a benevolent world where pleasure is not only possible, but our intimately experienced norm.

The pleasure of a sunset, a warm breeze, an icy snowflake, a full belly, our canine companion's exuberant, joyful greeting, and more, all confirm for us what our body experiences; the world is an okay place. From this orientation, when unfortunate, painful or even acutely stressful things happen, we are far more likely to take them in stride. We do not throw up our hands and say, "why do these things always happen to me?!" We feel the feelings which result from the event. We take this opportunity to re-affirm our sense of overall wellness and typically, eventually, we come back to the fundamental goodness of the world. In this way, we form adaptive habitual thinking that keeps us safe. Essentially, we become 'trauma-proof'. Our regular experience of, and trust in, pleasure are the essential ingredients in the neurological chemistry of a trauma-proof brain.

Yet one of the insidious byproducts of unsequenced trauma in a body is that, over time, the body can orient, more and more steadfastly, to the opposite belief about the world described above. Also called a 'negativity bias', in this orientation, the world *isn't* a benevolent place and things *don't* usually feel good. If we don't have a caring community to bring us back into the goodness of the world, to take us literally into their arms and remind us of our wellness and the world's wellness, and worse yet, if our community is responsible for the trauma in the first place, we learn to bypass the wondrous and beautiful as the neurology of our brains have us cataloging the myriad painful and unpleasant things that seem to be our lot. Vigilance and the expectation of pain, or at least *not* pleasure, become our baseline. We do not do this consciously. We do this habitually and unconsciously in order to keep ourselves safe. While we might be tempted to imagine this only describes a small portion of the most unfortunate people in the world, this would be an erroneous perspective. Thanks to monotheistic religion and capitalism, and the parent – patriarchy – these come from, I am describing a version of the majority of people living in industrialized culture. In my experience, the most effective escape route from the vigilance and negative focus associated with trauma is not through the neurology of talk and cognitive processing but rather, through the body and the healthy, generative neurology of pleasure, which offer a person somatic evidence of wellness and safety. With the powers of our endogenous chemistry in its arsenal of healing, a baseline experience of pleasure and joy over time, coupled with the opportunity to sequence the thwarted responses to the original assaults, will slowly unwind even the most traumatized body.

WORKING WITH TRAUMA

The philosophy guiding somatic sex education starts with the assumption that our bodies orient toward health. Like a plant continually turning toward the sun, we are continually trying to find health. As practitioners, it's important that we also realize that even when a person behaves in a way that is currently maladaptive, it is coming from their desire for wholeness. Whatever maladaptive behavior they're doing is simply their best attempt in the moment at wellness. Somatic sex education starts with the belief that not only do we long to, but *we are designed to,* feel whole, to experience connection and pleasure. Many of us believe that this fundamental pleasure and wellness is a strong evolutionary function which, if supported, serves to keep us safe, emotionally and physically resilient and intelligently connected with one another.

It is important for us to remember that each harmful or destructive behavior, symptom or belief/story we see in our clients (especially clients who hold unsequenced trauma in their bodies) is actually a logical response to an experience of on-going lack of safety and wellness. At one point, that lack of safety and wellness was a measurable and objective reality. That it is no longer true (that there is no current or imminent threat) is a luxury of perception their ANS does not have. Their perceptions and behaviors are not pathological. They are simply stuck in a habitual loop of fear and threat, likely so familiar to them they see it as not only normal but necessary.

It is a critical and unique skill in our profession that we are curious and open-minded about all that we experience in our clients. A particular desire, turn-on or emotion are powerful clues for us to get to learn the unique landscape inhabited by each of our clients. The same is true for symptoms of un-integrated trauma. A seemingly frantic recoil to a particular type of touch, or a moment of panic in response to our voice sounding deeper than usual, are critical clues that will assist us in helping our clients understand more of the original story of their trauma. Training ourselves to pay close attention to a client's present state of being will also help us to become more trauma-informed, sensitive and aware for, and highly attuned to, this person and all the rest to come. It is our responsibility to educate ourselves here.

The basic principles of trauma work elegantly overlap with our work as somatic sex educators. Below, I describe some of the core principles of any work which desires to create a safe and inviting space for our clients to experience themselves, their wounds and wholeness and equally important, their essence or soul. It also happens that these core principles help to create an environment in which unsequenced trauma can be excavated, remembered, embodied and, eventually, integrated. For each principle I provide a brief description and follow with information on 1) how we might model these practices with and for our clients and 2) how we might invite our clients into these practices.

Be Here Now –

Being present to our current experience is at the very foundation of our capacity to heal from trauma events. Without this fundamental musculature and skill we can't begin to unwind the ravages of the past because we are constantly fielding the damaging perception that we are *still there*. As somatic sex educators, teaching presence is a fundamental part of our work. We teach the basic workings of mindfulness and presence, assisting our clients to build skills and tools which allow them to be more embodied, more present to their felt in-the-moment experiences, without judgment. This is a core tenet of trauma work.

Working Examples:

a. We are in a powerful position to permission presence by taking good care of ourselves and valuing our needs in sessions. We can pay attention to our breath, move slowly, share what is alive for us when appropriate, and model valuing what is true for us in how we speak of it.

b. A very helpful way to bring this core principle into our practice is by inviting each client to start their session with a silent few moments or even minutes, during which time they are eminently permissioned to go inward (if they feel comfortable they can close their eyes) and quiet their mind to the extent that it's possible, eventually gently scanning the body for what is apparent. No judgment needed, just a wonderful open invitation to notice what's there.

Acceptance, Non-Judgment & Integration

Learning to be truly mindful and present requires that we acknowledge what *is* without story or judgment. In trauma work, a necessary step in our healing is learning the skill of noticing and acknowledging without assigning value or story to the information or experience. We are taught to judge our emotions and experience, placing them in categories of 'good' or 'bad' from very early in our development. We are taught that happiness is a 'good' experience and sadness is a 'bad' one. We can help our clients learn to feel equanimity and curiosity regarding all information that arises from their inner inquiries. Here, we are assisting clients to excavate, acknowledge and care for all aspects of themselves without shame, shoulds or story. As with many of these principles, you will notice that learning to listen to and acknowledge our experience without judgment and shame is at odds with the fundamental teachings of industrialized culture. Monotheistic religion and capitalism both have, at their core, a belief that we are shameful and flawed. Inviting all our clients into mindful equanimity is a subversive act, helping them to become more trauma-resilient and emotionally sovereign in general. But beware – this is no place for trite affirmations, superficial mantras or anything of the sort. Learning to love ourselves despite the (sometimes abusive and life threatening) messages we received to the contrary as children is a fierce, arduous task. Often times we are the very last ones to accept aspects of our psyche that were so un-welcomed in the world as we were growing up.

Working examples:

a. We can model this skill for our clients by behaving generously with ourselves. This could look like caring for the ideas and thoughts that arise in each session, whether or not they 'land' with our clients. Modeling acceptance and non-judgment in this way will assist our clients to take more risks with their own creative ideas as they arise in sessions and in the larger world.

b. We help our clients learn this behavior by inviting them to self-reflect, helping them take the time required to do so – often vastly more time than they give themselves permission to take – and then slowly valuing each of their responses. When and if judgment arises as they speak their experience, we can, with gentle curiosity, ask questions that help bring awareness to any shame or story they may carry. All of this is slow and without judgment. It is all too easy to judge a person's judgment of themselves, and in doing so, of course, we've just confirmed their own internalized beliefs.

Safety First

We cannot begin to unravel trauma until we feel safe enough to do so. The body and psyche are brilliant and adaptive and are dedicated to keeping our most precious parts safely sequestered until we can be certain of safety. Safety is a moving target however, and often we have to engage in a series of trial and error exercises whose consequences are relatively benign, in order to know when we're *just safe enough* to indulge a risky impulse toward our own health. Assisting clients to redefine their experience in their bodies, that the body can be a place of safety, authenticity, integrity and 'home', is a cornerstone practice for both trauma and somatic sex education practitioners. It is ESSENTIAL that the clients be empowered to learn how to create safety in their environments. Part of our responsibility as practitioners is knowing exactly how we contribute to either the experience of a safe environment or a dangerous threatening one. Things like prosody (the tone, speed and sound of our voice as encouraging, gentle and welcoming, or not), being aware of our facial affect (expressions) both contribute to our own sense of safety (that *we* feel in *our* bodies) as well as how our clients feel in theirs. Here, again, we must understand and be sensitive to the various ways our clients tell us how safe (or not) they feel. They may be largely unconscious to their experience of disregulation. They may be so accustomed to a baseline sense of threat and lack of safety that if you were to take their word for it, you would assume they were just fine. When, in fact, they may be terrified. We are wise to learn how our own gestures, sounds, language, breathing speed and more can and do contribute to our clients' increasing sense of wellness and safety *or* the opposite.

Working Examples:
a. We can model this skill with our clients by adjusting the room as needed when we notice something not quite right. We can also

speak to the care we have for our own sense of safety when we are startled by something or caught off-guard. A word about valuing our own importance: I remember early in my practice, when I was a clinician in a busy inner-city teaching hospital, I was sitting with a young new mother who had lost her own mother, to whom she was very close, to a heart attack just days after her baby was born. She and I were the same age and I felt as adrift in my skills as she felt bereft in her life. In the middle of a session one day a 'code blue' was called over the intercom, which signaled that someone had gone into cardiac arrest and staff was being summoned. I was fairly new at this job and 'code blue' was still a scary event for me. I paused for a moment to allow myself to feel the emotions that came up for me and she immediately noticed. Without even knowing what I was doing, I had given her a moment to refer back to and permission to find language around her own fear and sadness. From that moment on she used the term 'code blue' to give herself permission to stop and readjust, attune to herself and acknowledge her sense of grief and loneliness.

b. Well-known trauma therapist Pat Ogden, founder of the Sensorimotor Psychotherapy Institute, was the first practitioner to describe her work of inviting her clients to assess their experience of safety in her therapy room and rearrange furniture based on their experience of the room, including where Pat's chair sat and the direction it faced. She found that healing work of any sort cannot begin until a person is given permission to prioritize their safety. Of course, our physical surroundings are an important factor in our general experience of safety. She also found that often, when clients are given assisted permission to attend to themselves here, the work has already started. Invite your clients to look around the room, feel what feels good and safe and what feels off. Invite them to rearrange the room, including your position and theirs. With each new shift, ask them how it feels to them. Invite them to try different arrangements and share the experience they have of each one. This can be a place of creativity and play as well as a place of care and intention. Occasionally, you might encounter a person for whom the bold maneuver of moving *your* office (and perhaps even you!) around is simply too confronting. It takes a certain level of safety to engage in the process of exploring our interior experience to survey 'Am I safe here? What could I do to be more safe?' You might find a client unable to participate in the full exercise. If this happens invite them to choose where they would like to sit. Once seated, invite them to look around the room, taking time to breath and notice their body state, sensations and emotions to whatever level they can. Invite them to point out pleasing or dis-pleasing things and places in the room.

Education Is Power!

As somatic sex educators we understand that education is powerful; knowing what is possible and why it's possible is profoundly inspiring and often the biggest single thing we provide for our clients. This is another great confluence between our work and trauma integration work. Becoming educated around what's possible, what's happening, what *could* happen and *why* it happens for a person in the grips of un-sequenced trauma is often a gift of liberation impossible to describe. Just as we do educate them around the arc of their arousal, the breath that facilitates and prolongs it, the myriad factors that might limit the neurology of their pleasure and more, helping our clients understand how a body and brain innately respond to trauma, what is actually happening for them, and how they can effect a different outcome with mindfulness and practice, is an extraordinary gift of efficacy we can offer each and every client we see. In addition, we have the possibility of normalizing the behavioral by-products of trapped trauma in a body, which assist our clients in letting go of shame, self-blame and judgment.

Working Examples:

a. As practitioners we can model a regard for education and let our clients know we value supportive information, which helps us cultivate increased intimacy with our experience. We can offer examples from our own lives when a particular experience arises for our clients with which we have familiarity.

b. When our client is struggling with a particular experience, we have the great opportunity to go to the book shelf, grab just the right book and find the diagram that puts an overwhelming subjective experience into brilliant and logical order. When it comes to trauma trapped in the body we are, in many ways, merely mammals and a certain universality exists among us all. Normalization of responses and experiences that often seem big and out of our control can provide a powerful first step in our clients' wellness.

The Importance of Play

Somatic sex educators know how critical it is that our innocent, creative and in some cases undaunted playful parts be nurtured and invited into our generative sexual worlds. In trauma work it is no different. It is often these very aspects that were silenced and eventually sequestered because it was no longer safe to let them remain openly in the world. Additionally, many of us find that it is also these very sequestered parts that will lead us courageously into creative healing opportunities. Yet creativity cannot happen in a field of danger. Creativity is a luxury when it comes to survival. And perhaps many of us have experienced this in our own lives. When we are afraid or in shock, we are least capable of thinking creatively. In teaching the importance of play, talk is cheap. We want to embody playfulness and invite it into our offices.

Working Examples:

a. Those of us who already have a relationship with humor, whimsy and play will merely need permission to not hold back when it comes to our interactions with our clients. Even if it appears to fall 'flat', we can check in with them about what it was like to experience us in this place of grounded levity. Often, our playful parts are like animals who have rightly taken cover behind the safest tree. It takes repeated invitations and lots of patience to have our playful parts feel safe enough to venture back out into the open.

b. We can invite play directly into our sessions by actually playing with our clients! This is not rocket science. Though we want to stay deeply attuned to our clients' experience, we can bring a gentle humor to our way of being with them. We can bring more generously joyful expressions to our facial responses. We can take joy in their presence with us. And if we have the luxury of practicing with animals in the room (I practice with two dogs and two cats) we can always rely on the intelligence of animals to bring levity, softness and playfulness into the sessions.

Creating Secure Attachment In Our Relationships With Clients

For a more in-depth conversation about Attachment please see the 'Attachment, Attunement & Neurobiology' handbook. 'Attachment' refers to the health of the original bond we form with a caregiver in our infancy and childhood. 'Attunement' refers to the interpersonal (and intrapersonal) process of acknowledging, understanding and valuing ours or another's current experience. Humans and certain other mammal species are endowed with neurological capacities, including mirror neurons, which allow us to intuit and empathize with each other's felt experiences. When we are attuning to a client, we might find ourselves shifting our facial expression, slowing our breath down, changing our prosody and even language. When we attune to our own or another's experience, we are acknowledging and making room for this experience without judgment or shaming. The developmental experience of being consistently attuned to, as a child, allows us to learn, as a first language, that the experiences, feelings and responses within our internal landscape are not only okay but valuable. Here we learn there is room for us in this world and that we matter enough that others will make room for us. It is in our earliest experiences of being attuned to that we create the important story of the universe that we are welcome and important, just as we are; we do not need to deny or alter our naturally occurring unique, sometimes inconvenient or messy, selfhood in order to be loved and accepted.

Our experience of attachment and attunement (or the lack thereof) significantly determines our capacity to create and sustain healthy intimacy with ourselves and others, throughout the rest of our lives. Having a working understanding of Attachment is, in my experience, part of the essential knowledge base we must cultivate and nourish if we are to be able to understand the myriad experiences our clients bring to us and inevitably act out with us, and if we are to rise to the potential we have as critical humans in their lives. We cannot touch our clients' most shamed, reviled, pleasure-filled, numbed-out, intimate geography and imagine we will remain outside the borders of a deeply intimate relationship with each of them. Whether we are with our clients for one session or forty, we are in a tremendously powerful position with our clients, to either ignorantly replicate fractured relationship patterns or offer our clients the opportunity to experience truly safe, generous intimacy with another. Creating a space of secure attachment with clients is a foundational piece of all trauma work. Again, we will not begin to allow the unfolding of old patterns and holding until we feel safe enough to do so. When our clients feel held in a field of regard, care and consistency, invited to bring all of themselves to the present moment, regardless of how loud, inconvenient, un-kempt or even critical, and we do not take it personally but rather welcome it all with curiosity and genuine attention, old patterns of fear begin to arise and unwind.

It is estimated that less than 5% of all children in the USA will experience secure attachment. It is up to us to know our own wounding here, so we do not inadvertently work our attachment patterns with our clients. And even more, it is our responsibility to know enough about what secure attachment and relating looks like to role model it with each of them. If you notice significant anxiety in yourself in response to certain clients who are late, who cancel sessions or who do not want to schedule as frequently as you might like (to name a few options), and you notice you lose your capacity to stay curious about what might be happening for your client here, you have likely stumbled into an area of your own attachment wounding that requires immediate attention. Because of the delicate, vulnerable nature of the work we do with clients, and the tremendous courage and longing for wholeness that is alive in each of them, it is critical we do our work here so we can be solid relational experiences of attunement, connection and repair for our people.

Working Examples:

a. We can model secure attachment with our clients by holding ourselves in the relationship with them even when they cannot hold regard for us. We can let them know when something feels hard without making our experience their responsibility. We can say things like, "I feel sad when you don't show up for our scheduled appointments. I look forward to our work together and deeply value the goals and visions you've shared with me here." We are modeling the vulnerability that is necessary for any relationship of secure attachment and intelligent intimacy. But we are not making our experience our client's responsibility to 'fix'. To do that would be to replicate what far too many of us experienced in our childhoods, where it became our responsibility to behave in ways that were acceptable and pleasing to our family system. It is never our client's responsibility to attend to our well-being, but it is critical, in our process of creating secure attachment and attunement with them, that they know their importance and their value. We are letting them know they are important enough to have an impact in our lives. Offering this without expectation or a need for our client to respond in any particular way is a gift many of us have not received in our lifetimes. When we offer a statement of this nature, it is important that we follow it up with an inquiry, 'How does it feel for you to hear me say that I value our work and you?'

b. Working with our clients to help them understand what they experienced in the realm of (in)secure attachment with their family of origin is a highly valuable discrete piece of work. It doesn't take long to help them draw the picture of their experience as a child, how well emotionally and physically held they were, how safe they felt to be truthful and authentic with the adults in their lives and how this all continues to play out in every relationship they (attempt to) cultivate in the present day.

Restoring Sovereignty, Agency & Power

One of the primary pillars of trauma work which, again, parallels our work as somatic sex educators is that we prioritize – in our every movement and every breath with every client – their internal musculature of agency, sovereignty, choice and power. One of the primary ways we do this is by learning the art of teaching, modeling, inviting, nurturing and patiently waiting for, enthusiastic consent in our clients. It is safe to say that most of our clients come through our door without ever having been given permission to have boundaries around sex. Most of us are taught *not* to have boundaries around our sexuality. We are told who we are from birth; we are conscripted to behave in very narrow and curated ways based on our perceived gender and way-of-being. Statistically, 35% of us, *regardless of gender,* are likely to have been assaulted in some form by the age of 35. In this reality we must see that many behaviors or actions we've been taught to negatively label might in reality be an attempt at agency. For instance, rather than a move away from one's impulse for wholeness, often times "resistance" is a hard-won attempt to create a necessary boundary. Given this reality, many of us can energetically nod our heads when asked if we feel empowered and sovereign when in reality, we might not truly know what it feels and looks like to authentically have choice and operate from this emancipated, whole position. Often we learn this alongside our clients. But it is safe to say they will not ever move into a relationship of empowerment with the events which traumatized them if we cannot help them develop the muscles of true agency in sessions with us. One decision at a time, one deeper breath at a time, one seemingly strange choice to skip an appointment, to talk for a whole session – one exertion of agency at a time, if we continue to stay with our clients, will have them moving into ever-more power over the forces which seemed so all-controlling at one time in their lives.

Working Examples:

a. A very great way to model agency and choice with our clients is by attending to our own needs in each session. We do this without making our needs our client's problem, or ever expecting them to take care of us. But we model the gentle honoring of our ergonomic comfort, our scheduling requirements, our fee and payment schedules and more. If we are not comfortable with our own sovereignty, if we are still working on the internal permission required to have boundaries, we will likely convey discomfort and perhaps even hostility toward our clients when we feel we've over-stepped our needs.

b. In session we can invite them to consider themselves and their desires at a much slower pace, helping them to acknowledge each internal message that arises, one at a time. Opportunities for this come in the smallest of places, perhaps around scheduling for example. We may notice our client is hesitating but we can't quite understand why. Here we can invite them to notice what is present in their bodies, and invite them to speak the associated stories that often come charging in to keep us in 'appeasement' mode when we fear reprisal for being honest.

Re-Connecting Mind & Body

One of the most powerful tools in the integration of still-living traumatic memories is the re-connection of mind, brain and body: helping to move the largely unconscious experiences our clients have of their trauma back into a cognitive order and integration. One of the intelligent byproducts of un-sequenced trauma in the body is that it often demands a dissociation of mind from body. We adaptively learn to disconnect what is happening in our bodies from our mind's innate capacity for and curiosity about self awareness. Yet as fortunate owners of the most advanced brain known to sentient life (though arguably we have yet to use it well!), we have the capacity to not only understand what our brain is up to in any given moment, but to help create and change our experience. We can assist clients in having an empowering objective experience of what is often a tyrannically subjective, disempowering experience of the physiological and emotional symptoms of unresolved trauma. Specifically, we can assist our clients to comprehend their formerly unconscious experience of neurological processes in any given moment and then, very powerfully, we can assist them to create different outcomes from seemingly hopeless dead-end feelings. I've encountered many a somatic practitioner who has a bias of body over mind and perhaps even a dismissal of the mind's great importance and power. But the mind is not an adversary when it comes to embodiment. As it is developed and harnessed in Industrial culture, it is certainly anathema to embodiment. Yet with the proper unlearning and diligent practice, we can begin to have an even deeper experience of embodiment if we learn to harness our mind in service to this task.

Working Examples:

a. We can model a mind-body connection for our clients when we carefully share with them our felt experience in the moment, in a way that uses both the superpower of the mind to organize and the superpower of the body to re-feel the experience we're speaking of. If we refuse to adopt the disembodied style of *talking about* a thing and instead speak in a way that allows a living experience complete with feelings and sensations, we are modeling a radical way of inclusivity that values the essential partnership of mind and body.

b. We can guide our clients toward this skill when, during our sessions, we ask them to slow down as they're *reporting* about an experience and invite them to pause and take a moment to see if there are any associated *feelings* linked to the words. We can invite them to weave the thoughts with the (often dissociated) feelings multiple times in a given conversation until, before we know it, they are doing this for themselves.

Naming & Celebrating The Good

Just like learning to allow pleasure to happen in our bodies, it is of great importance for those who are in the stronghold of un-integrated trauma that they learn how to notice what is right and good in the moment. It is an old-world vestige that our brains are better equipped to log a painful experience in our accessible memory than they are a pleasurable one. Some happiness researchers like Rick Hanson advise their clients to spend an extra fifteen seconds dwelling on happy or pleasurable experiences and thoughts because we are evolutionarily hard-wired to over-emphasize and remember scary, painful or unpleasant experiences. For a person who is struggling with unresolved trauma, it is likely they are even more attuned to negative input as they are likely consistently scanning their field for danger. Learning to name the good and pleasurable is part of a somatic sex educator's basic bag of tools. We often begin each session with a body scan or mindfulness practice of some sort, helping clients to notice exactly what is happening in their physical and emotional bodies; giving attention to when something feels peaceful, good, calm, painful, anxious and more. Helping our clients to orient to what *is* good in the body, what does feel good, whole and well is a necessary tool in the naming and integration of embodied trauma. And it may not be a dramatic 'ah-hah!' or even particularly welcome in the moment! Sometimes our client might be insistent that there is absolutely nothing that feels good ever. Sometimes, this might look like our client identifying that the last knuckle of their little finger on their left hand isn't numb, or doesn't have pain. This is a monumental beginning. Celebrate it with them.

Working Examples:

a. Modeling this for our clients can look quite seamless as we quietly celebrate what it feels like when the sun comes peering under the window sill and finds our face, or we breath deeply as we stretch in anticipation of a table session. Being alive and appreciative in our bodies is a powerful form of permission and modeling which is all-too-rare in our fast-paced disembodied cultures.

b. As already mentioned, something as simple as a body scan can allow a client to slow down long enough to (sometimes even begrudgingly) admit there is pleasure in their body. But even when there isn't something as marvelous as pleasure, it is equally important to help our clients understand that all sensation can be regarded as good, since regardless of whether the sensation is pleasurable or not, it carries information vital to our well-being and experience of intimacy with self.

Embodied Memory & Pleasure
Learning to Turn Toward Pleasure as Healing & Medicine

It is a primary value we hold as Somatic Sex Educators that our pleasure is vastly more important than merely a thing that has us *feel good*. We understand it to be a source of limitless healing and wellness. And far more than the process of pleasure that happens in our orgasm alone, we know and teach our clients to experience the subtleties of pleasure within the wide range found when we acknowledge both down-regulated and up-regulated, relaxed and aroused energy states. With trauma work, it's critical to see the confluence here. Interestingly, the human body was designed to withstand and process quite a range of complex acute events of substantial shock; a natural disaster, a deadly threat from an animal or aggressor, the death of a loved one. Certainly any of these events can cause a body to hold unsequenced trauma. But equally as important is the awareness that our nervous system is *not designed* to cope with what has become a fairly ubiquitous human experience and certainly is a keystone experience for those with unsequenced trauma in their systems; the effects of *daily, on-going unmitigated stress*. "The stress-response can become more damaging than the stressor itself. Stress-related diseases and psychological uproar emerge by continually turning on a physiological system that has evolved for responding to acute physical emergencies" rather than the on-going pervasive nervous system revving that is stress (Sapolskly, 2004 as quoted in Haines, 2014).

In our work inviting bodies and souls back into equilibriums of resiliency and health, implementing body-based experiences for our clients – and the use of embodied memory and specific invitations to embody safety and wellness – can be efficient and powerful.

As discussed previously, embodied memories are the pre-cognitive (or *beyond* the mind) memories stored in the tissue and cells of our bodies which get triggered through gestures, expressions, sensory input and, importantly, when our bodies are touched. Many somatic sex educators have learned to be on the lookout for these embodied memories, trusting implicitly their veracity and importance. Academic research and theory know very little about this type of memory given that, in keeping with the patriarchal emphasis on cerebral cognition over embodied intelligence, few studies have been done. However, the study of epigenetics has illuminated an undeniable process; environmental stress on the gestating mother can cause living trauma not only to the fetuses she carries but the eggs within those female fetuses. That an acute event does not require cognitive awareness in order to cause on-going physiological and emotional trauma in individuals for generations upon generations is the bad news. The good news is that the very same systems and mechanisms that allow for this damage, allow for the identification and healing of the trauma as well. Somatic sex educators are, in fact, at the front lines of this miraculous healing as we work with the body to remember, and orient to, pleasure of all kinds. The slow, moment-to-moment, shifts that a body undergoes to accommodate more possibility that the world is a benevolent place; that our bodies are designed as much for on-going states of pleasure and joy as they are designed to respond in the presence of an acute threat.

Perhaps some of you have already discovered one byproduct of embodied memory at work when clients report anxiety around certain sensations and events routinely associated with pleasure. Often, an increased heart rate is an unavoidable physiological occurrence when we are sexually aroused. As a function controlled by the SNS, it does not necessarily discriminate between reasons for the arousal; that's the mind's job. However, if the mind has been in a constant state of vigilance as a result of unsequenced trauma, an increased heart rate is typically not a cause for celebration but rather panic. And the body that experiences this anxiety will likely not venture into arousal without trepidation. Trepidation around arousal might begin to look like avoidance, which might eventually become an inability to find arousal. In my practice, I would venture to say that, when I work with women who cannot find their arousal and orgasm, it is because feelings of anxiety and or fear have been coupled with the physiological state of arousal, and the wild, unpredictable and often out of control qualities associated with this terrain. And so it is with male-bodied men who come in to see me because they are concerned about the functioning of their penises. A penis that does not behave according to the culture's unrealistic (I would add, pathological and oppressive) standards can be a traumatizing experience in itself for many men (and sometimes their partners, too!), who are offered little if any diversity in the way masculine sexuality is allowed to show up. If the phallus does not get hard with the slightest breeze of provocation, and stay hard for hours on end, a man runs the risk of what might turn into debilitating shame and ridicule from himself and others.

In these examples arousal has been linked, in the body and the brain, to states of anxiety and fear. This feedback loop is common. It is often the case that the feelings of anxiety and fear carry with them volumes of loud stories; information from lived experiences when acute events were left unacknowledged, leading to unsequenced trauma in the body. Much of the time, these acute events are not cognitively acknowledged. But the link is indelible: increased heart rate = arousal = feelings of shame, anxiety = a lack of safety. Arousal and its associated spectrum of physiological embodied states can trigger the brain to respond with a tidal wave of information based on events and consequences that have been stored as consolidated memory in relation to the simple and oft-occurring physiological experience of an increased heart rate.

We can help clients unwind these associations, and literally re-write consolidated memory, by creating safe(er) space for them to intentionally explore these states of embodiment. Simple practices like sensate focus, where we invite a client to touch their body for their own pleasure, are magnificent places to start. While going very slow, and slower still, we invite our client to focus on the awareness of the sensation in their fingertips and in their forearm while also noticing how they are breathing and sitting/lying. We can gently bring their attention to their facial expression. If, during the practice, they arrive at a place that feels *good*, we can invite them to notice what their facial expression *feels* like. If they are grimacing or frozen here (because their pleasure may be associated with anxiety and fear) we can invite them to try a more neutral expression. We might even have them try a gentle smile or other expression indicating pleasure. Here, we can assist clients to re-write stored memories by revisiting them and shifting the states of embodiment that have become customarily associated with those experiences. An important distinction here is that we are not overriding their experience, or making their current experience wrong. We are helping them bring curiosity and awareness to an unconsciously engrained way of being that limits their capacity to be well. We are doing this so they may, more gracefully and regularly, access experiences of embodied pleasure and wellness.

The Role of Orgasmic Energy in Assisting Trauma Sequencing
Learning to Use The Orgasm Cycle to Assist Clients' Sequencing of Trauma

Orgasm energy is the energy of completion, of full sequence. Most of us know the experience of both physiological and neurological frustration which occurs for us when we (believe we) are heading blissfully and assuredly toward an orgasm, and something happens. Perhaps we remember something ultimately distracting, like an event the next day that we're nervous about. Perhaps we experience something in our body which then places a story in our mind, a story we cannot un-think in our attempt to get back on our orgasmic track. Conversely we also likely know the marvelous experience of the benevolence of our body to bring us to the promised land of full orgasm. The embodied, emotional and physical experience of our orgasm is an energetic experience of completion. Unlike so many other experiences, it is a full and complete cycle which includes our preliminary resting state, into desire (or arousal), then arousal (or desire), then a building which results in a peak moment, which then restores us to a resting place. By no means universal, many people describe something of a universal experience in this cycle, of excitement, plateau, orgasm and resolution (which is the language developed by the original Western culture orgasm pioneers Masters & Johnson). The use of the word 'resolution' is problematic in one sense; that it conveys there is something to be *resolved* (like an issue, dilemma or problem). It is problematic because it further supports an erroneous and harmful thing many of us are taught, that our desire and longing is a thing to be managed and dealt with rather than a marvelous, fertile and discrete experience in itself. However, energetically, physiologically, many would describe our experience in the plateau phase of our sexual arousal as something that very distinctly seems to need to move to a conclusion. This experience of *resolution* then, can be well utilized – reverently put to good use – when it comes to the experience of unsequenced trauma.

Unsequenced trauma can often feel like stuck energy akin to the experience we have when our arousal gets hijacked before we reach orgasm. Many of us have gotten to the point of intellectually knowing *about* our trauma, even feeling certain emotions associated with the original event, but still feeling as if we have not moved through a full sequencing of the stuck energy and stories.

Let's use a specific example: For one year of regular sessions I worked with a woman in her mid fifties, a seasoned psychotherapist, who had come to see me because she had "tried everything" to unwind the trauma associated with the repeated childhood sexual abuse of her father and older brother. Like so many adults of childhood sexual abuse, for decades she had been unable to feel anything below her solar plexus and above her knees. She had pursued a certification in yoga instruction and had become a pillar in her local contact improvisation community (which relies on deep embodiment and presence). She had studied meditation for three decades and was a daily practitioner. She had gotten to the point in her work where she was gracefully able to feel the specific emotional and physiological experiences associated with her early experience as a young girl and adolescent. She was able to speak to these experiences, to let a certain amount of movement and embodiment accompany her more cerebral understanding of her emotional experiences.

But here she "stalled out" as she would put it. Perhaps most painfully and intolerably for her, she could not feel the caring, gentle devoted touch of her partner of three decades when she would caress and hold her genitals. She was able to experience orgasm but as she described it, it was a fast and furious thing; a thing that felt fleeting and "unhelpful". For years as a younger woman, she was delighted by how easily she could get aroused and orgasm. But upon entering her late forties she realized she wasn't actually present for these experiences. She likened it to riding a roller coaster and not breathing, squeezing her eyes closed the whole time – "What kind of a ride is *that?!*" she longingly and frustratingly exclaimed. She felt stuck in this place, not able to move past this particular experience in her body, to a place where it felt like a full sequence of the trauma moved through her; a sequence to which she could be utterly present. Much like we might describe the frustration of getting so close to orgasm and then being thwarted, so would she describe her experience with her trauma work and the lack of fullness and depth in her pleasure.

After many months in our work, building a ground of health, trust and safety, we had moved to a place where she was experiencing forty-five (or more) minutes of pleasure. Pleasure for which she was completely present, able to gently talk to herself during her experience, describing her sensations and any related embodied memories that would predictably arrive at certain moments when certain tender geographies of her body would be touched. She was able to let the tears and powerlessness of the young girl of her move through her. She was able to let her rage and her

"No! You cannot touch me! I am not yours to touch!" move through her and audibly out into the room. She was able to reclaim her eros, her sensuality and her actual physical landscape for her own pleasure. She was able to pause her own arousal when she felt required to establish a boundary. At these times she might actually stand up, on the table, in order to express her adult sovereign woman, in protection of her little girl. And with all this, one day, she was finally able to harness her intact deep orgasm response with the desire for her own wholeness, to bring a cycle of completion to her heretofore unsequenced trauma.

In one unforgettable session, a session we had been imagining and talking about for many weeks, she was able to speak to and through the repeated violations at the hands of her father and brother, while continuously reclaiming her own body and pleasure for herself. As she moved closer and closer to orgasm (a thing she had, in the past, only been able to allow by not breathing and "checking out") she was able to slow down, pause, breathe deeply, establish her safety then claim her pleasure more, speaking her gratitude for her body and its wholeness, tears and laughter weaving together, moans of pleasure and fierce screams, protecting her borders, intermingling as gracefully as smoke sensuously moves through air. Here, she came into and through her full orgasm, as the orgasm diligently and meticulously brought all the unresolved, unsequenced trauma with it.

Resourcing Exercises To Build Ground Of Health In Our Clients

Even if we are working with clients whose resiliency seems strong, who have miraculously managed to avoid any overtly traumatizing experiences, we might still want to be utilizing some tools which serve to build ground of health, more resiliency and a greater sense of invitation and permission in their relationship with us. Below is a short list of some fun practices and games we can do with our clients that might just stir up some interesting experiences and information for everyone! In each example the practice or game is interesting in and of itself, but it is also very important to leave plenty of time to talk about what comes up for them as a result of the experience.

a. Invite your client to set an arbitrary boundary, to practice saying, "NO!" and using their body to dramatize what "NO" might *look like*, without words. Stop frequently during this exercise to make room for them to share their experience. Is there anything that would make "No!" more forthcoming? Would it help them to see you model it? A word about "no": Our true "no" can only be authentically accessed if we've managed to cultivate an internal adult or sovereign aspect. For those of us who were taught (by words or actions) that our own boundaries were unacceptable, we must work in our adulthood to cultivate an internal 'parent' figure who can establish and maintain boundaries. This doesn't happen by mimicking "no!" It happens by slowly, but surely, learning that we can keep ourselves safe in the presence of our own boundary establishment. Bringing consciousness and words to this process for our clients is essential.

b. Invite your client to use their physical might to push against a wall, or you (if that feels safe to you both). Check in with them: "what does it feel like to use your force? How much of your body (ask for a percentage) is allowed to participate? Is there anything holding you back? Where do you feel it? What would help give it permission to take a break?"

c. We often invite our clients to savor a particularly pleasurable moment, but it's part of our resiliency, and Peter A. Levine's exercise of 'pendulation' to be able to lean into a moment that isn't necessarily pleasurable, as long as the client is bolstered by a sense of safety. If your client is having an experience that is *not* pleasant (but not acutely awful), invite them to take a second or two (or longer, if they want) to bring more curiosity to the sensation, location and experience. Make sure to invite them to speak to what they notice about their curiosity itself (did it grow, did it disappear...?) as much as what they noticed about the sensation, its intensity, location etc. Often, when we allow a gentle curiosity and attention to fall onto a sensation that isn't pleasant, we find it shifts, lessens and otherwise changes. Our experience of ourselves often shifts as well.

d. At times when your client seems to be in a greater state of anxiety, stress, sadness or fear, invite them to think of a person or animal to whom they feel close, and from whom they derive comfort, in their current dayworld life. Then have them imagine this close companion right by their side in the moment. Slow them down here and have them breathe into their abdomen and belly to assist their nervous system's automatic relaxation response. Have them imagine the heat of that one's body, the sound of their breathing. Let them feel this experience for a few moments and invite them to notice how they feel now in relation to the anxiety, sadness or fear.

e. Whenever a client seems to be slipping in and out of presence, especially when they're on the table, eyes shut – which can be a particularly difficult place to discern their level of dissociation vs pleasurable trance – if you're concerned they are slipping in and out of a trauma state, gently invite them to *pendulate* between their *away* state and the present moment by having them gently open their eyes and reference the room, you, the light on the walls, the day of the week and other present moment realities. They can move back and forth in the pendulation for quite some time, slowly building the musculature of conscious curation of presence and grounding.

f. If your client is on the table and you're sensing they could use some help staying in the present moment, whether they're having difficulty staying present to a 'bossy massage' or seem to be slipping away from their body and sensation during a Taoist erotic massage-style session, invite them to place their own hand on their body, perhaps over their heart, on their abdomen or on their third eye/pituitary gland. Ask them what they notice here, in the space between their skin of the palm of their hand and the skin of the place on their body they are touching.

g. A fun game to play with our clients is to rotate our location and positions around the room. I have done this with clients during intake sessions, where we'll start in chairs then move to the floor under the window, then move to the carpet, then over to meditation cushions. I invite them to take over and call out the places we'll move next. We don't move frantically, but sometimes we do end up a bit breathless. In a particularly interesting session I had a young woman request (as if her little girl was deliciously doing something she knew was against the rules) that we race out to the field behind my home office. We did…running the whole way. When she got there she fell into the field on her back, throwing her arms up and said, "Oh! *This* is my definition of ecstasy!" I would never have known this, had we not played that game. This information that I learned about her on the first day became an essential piece of our journey together and her journey into her wholeness.

CONCLUSION:
TRAUMA-INFORMED PRACTICE

Having a 'trauma-informed' practice *does not* mean you've taken it upon yourself to become one of the world's leading trauma authorities. Having a trauma-informed practice *does* means you've educated yourself on the prevalence, signs and symptoms of trauma, as well as some of the many options when it comes to its treatment.

A trauma-informed practice means you have taken into consideration the ways a person with unsequenced trauma in their body might *feel* in your presence, in your physical office and with your touch. And in that process, you have modified your behaviors, physical environments, your processes and protocols according to your findings, and your clients' feedback.

A trauma-informed practice means we have learned how to spot the living effects of trauma in a human body, to assess when a client is in acute distress and in need of more specific professional support and how to, above all, create a space and a way-of-being in our practices where we are eminently careful of and sensitive to the many ways trauma shows up and can be triggered. This is, fundamentally, the core of a trauma-informed practice.

A trauma-informed practitioner is one who is informed by, and stays current with, the basic information regarding trauma, its symptoms, triggers and treatments. And, just as critical, a trauma-informed practitioner is one who is animated by a supple responsiveness, conscious to the myriad ways a traumatized body responds, moment by moment, to its environment. This practitioner has taken care to know and unwind their own unsequenced trauma so it does not unconsciously derail their capacity to hold eminent safety, boundaries and awareness with all clients who place their bodies and souls in the practitioner's hands.

Perhaps most importantly, a trauma-informed practitioner is one who prioritizes a consistent council of their peers and mentors/elders. This is a pioneering, young and edgy field, one which is fraught with the possibility of encountering our own, and our clients', shadow parts. It is incumbent upon us to create and maintain regular peer supervision groups as well as finding mentors and elders whom we trust.

Through consistently more sophisticated practices of attunement, we can become practitioners who *cognitively feel* the current physio-emotional states of our clients – perhaps before even they are consciously aware of them. We can learn to honor and respect our embodied experiences as we also consistently learn to become more subtly aware of the ways our presence impacts others.

The more we become astute, attuned practitioners, the more we facilitate the human work of our time; our human healing and wholing so that future generations may see a species of humans organized around well-being and care rather than inequity and injustice.

BIBLIOGRAPHY

Haines, Steve. *Trauma Is Really Strange*. London ; Philadelphia: Singing Dragon, 2015.

Hanson, Rick. *Hardwiring Happiness: How to Reshape Your Brain and Your Life*. Rider, 2014.

Levine, Peter A. *In an Unspoken Voice: How the Body Releases Trauma and Restores Goodness*. Berkeley: North Atlantic Books, U.S., 2010.

— — —. *Trauma and Memory: Brain and Body in a Search for the Living Past: A Practical Guide for Understanding and Working with Traumatic Memory*. Berkeley, California: North Atlantic Books, U.S., 2015.

— — —. *Waking The Tiger: Healing Trauma – The Innate Capacity To Transform Overwhelming Experiences*. Berkeley, California: North Atlantic Books, U.S., 1997.

Minton, Kekuni, Pat Ogden, Clare Pain, Daniel J. Siegel, and Bessel Van Der Kolk. *Trauma and the Body: A Sensorimotor Approach to Psychotherapy*. 1 edition. New York: W. W. Norton & Company, 2006.

Porges, Stephen. *The Polyvagal Theory: Neurophysiological Foundations of Emotions, Attachment, Communication, and Self-Regulation*. New York: W. W. Norton & Company, 2011.

van der Kolk, Bessel. *The Body Keeps the Score: Brain, Mind, and Body in the Healing of Trauma*. Reprint edition. New York, NY: Penguin Books, 2015.

TRAININGS

Bridging Soma & Soul – a unique 9-month training created by seasoned trauma practitioners Dr. Sweigh Spilkin and Katie Asmus. This training supports practitioners to "tap into the brilliance of the brain and nervous system and teach you hands-on tools to help your clients heal, evolve, and thrive…Bridging Soma & Soul is an opportunity to integrate different schools of learning to bring out your unique gifts." For more details: http://www.thresholdshealing.com/bss/

ABOUT THE AUTHOR

Christiane Pelmas has been in the business of sitting with people – in circles, dyads, community groups and more – since 1984. A clinical social worker, psychotherapist and somatic sex educator by training in her current life, in past lives she has been an assistant vice-president of a Fortune 100 venture capital firm, a graphic designer for start-ups and the natural foods industry and an exotic dancer. Through it all she has been a mother, activist, poet, gardener and writer. As she moves into mid-life she continues sitting with people in her private practice in Boulder, Colorado, writing, teaching, supervising and mentoring, and enjoying life with her vital community, including a beautiful gift of a partner, and two wild adult sons, other precious humans, some extraordinary animals and the wild creatures, fields and mountains of the landscape they all call home.

Christiane's endeavors come from a deep and unyielding desire to encounter and feed soul; the shy, voracious, genuine creature at the core of our being. Right now, it is our nourished and courageous souls that The World is most hungry for, and in desperate need of.

www.christianepelmas.com

Other publications include *The Women's Wisdom Guidebook & Card Deck*

Ways To Work With Christiane

If you'd like more of Christiane you can hire her for speaking, workshops, trainings and consulting. She runs on-going group and individual supervision and teaches continuing education for somatic sex educators, erotic body workers, sex workers, traditional body workers, health-care professionals and psychotherapists. Please send all inquiries to christianepelmas@gmail.com.

Made in the USA
Middletown, DE
25 November 2019